RAY BRADBURY'S THE MARTIAN CHRONICLES

THE AUTHORIZED ADAPTATION

DENNIS CALERO

INTRODUCTION BY RAY BRADBURY

A NOVEL GRAPHIC FROM HILL AND WANG

A DIVISION OF FARRAR, STRAUS AND GIROUX
NEW YORK

To the ladies in my life,
Kris and Paloma
—Dennis Calero

HILL AND WANG
A DIVISION OF FARRAR, STRAUS AND GIROUX
18 WEST 18TH STREET, NEW YORK 10011

THIS IS A Z FILE, INC. BOOK
THE MARTIAN CHRONICLES COPYRIGHT © 1946, 1948, 1949, 1950, 1958 BY RAY BRADBURY,
RENEWED © 1977 BY RAY BRADBURY
INTRODUCTION COPYRIGHT © 2011 BY RAY BRADBURY
ARTWORK COPYRIGHT © 2011 BY DENNIS CALERO
ALL RIGHTS RESERVED
DISTRIBUTED IN CANADA BY D&M PUBLISHERS, INC.
PRINTED IN THE UNITED STATES OF AMERICA
PUBLISHED SIMULTANEOUSLY IN HARDCOVER AND PAPERBACK
FIRST EDITION, 2011

LIBRARY OF CONGRESS CATALOGING-IN-PUBLICATION DATA
CALERO, DENNIS
  RAY BRADBURY'S THE MARTIAN CHRONICLES : THE AUTHORIZED ADAPTATION/
DENNIS CALERO ; INTRODUCTION BY RAY BRADBURY. — 1ST ED.
    P. CM.
  ISBN 978-0-8090-6793-0 (HARDCOVER : ALK. PAPER) — ISBN 978-0-8090-8045-8
(PBK : ALK. PAPER).
  1. GRAPHIC NOVELS I. BRADBURY, RAY, 1920- MARTIAN CHRONICLES. II. TITLE.
III. TITLE: MARTIAN CHRONICLES
PN6727.C26R39 2011
741.5'973—DC22
                                                                    2011005169

ART BY DENNIS CALERO
EDITED BY HOWARD ZIMMERMAN
DESIGNED BY DEAN MOTTER

CONTRIBUTING ARTISTS:
"THE OFF SEASON": JOE ST. PIERRE
"THE MILLION-YEAR PICNIC": JOSH ADAMS
"THE EARTH MEN": JAMES SMITH

DIAGRAMATICS BASED ON OBSERVATIONS BY GIOVANNI SCHIAPARELLI, CIRCA 1877

WWW.FSGBOOKS.COM

1   3   5   7   9   10   8   6   4   2

CONTENTS

INTRODUCTION

BY RAY BRADBURY

WHEN I WAS SIX YEARS OLD I LIVED ON A STREET IN TUCSON, ARIZONA: LOWELL AVENUE. WHEN I'D BEEN THERE FOR A FEW MONTHS I DISCOVERED THAT IT HAD BEEN NAMED FOR PERCIVAL LOWELL, WHO WAS THE PHOTOGRAPHER OF MARS. I SAW PHOTOGRAPHS THAT HE MADE OF THE PLANET AND WAS INTRIGUED BY THE FACT THAT I LIVED ON THE STREET NAMED FOR HIM.

WHEN I WAS TEN YEARS OLD I BEGAN TO READ THE BOOKS OF EDGAR RICE BURROUGHS. I FELL IN LOVE WITH *JOHN CARTER, WARLORD OF MARS* AND *THUVIA, MAID OF MARS* AND EVERYTHING ELSE THAT HAD TO DO WITH THE PLANET MARS. I TOOK THE ADVICE OF JOHN CARTER WHEN I WAS TWELVE YEARS OLD. HE SAID, "GO OUT ON THE LAWN AT NIGHT AND LOOK UP AT THE RED PLANET IN THE SKY AND SAY, MARS, TAKE ME HOME."

THAT AUTUMN IN 1932 I THOUGHT THAT I'D TRY JUST THAT AND WENT OUT ON THE LAWN AND SHOUTED, "MARS, TAKE ME HOME!" IT TOOK ME HOME AND I STAYED THERE FOREVER.

THAT SAME WEEK I HAD AN ENCOUNTER WITH MR. ELECTRICO, WHO TOLD ME TO LIVE FOREVER.

I TOOK HIS ADVICE, AS WELL AS JOHN CARTER'S, AND THAT VERY WEEK I DID MY FIRST WRITING ON A TYPEWRITER.

JOHN CARTER CHANGED MY LIFE AND HERE IS THE PROOF. HERE IS THE PLANET MARS, LAID OUT FOR YOU TO READ.

IN MY TWENTIES I WROTE A SERIES OF SHORT STORIES, WHICH I SOLD FOR FANTASTIC SUMS ($20–30!) TO MAGAZINES CALLED *WONDER STORIES* AND *PLANET STORIES*.

I WROTE ALMOST DAILY ABOUT THE PLANET MARS AND DURING THAT TIME I MET A PRODUCER/DIRECTOR OF RADIO PROGRAMS, NORMAN CORWIN. ONE EVENING AT DINNER I TOLD HIM A STORY THAT I HAD WRITTEN ABOUT A WOMAN NAMED YLLA, MY MARTIAN MAIDEN, WHO HAD DREAMS ABOUT EARTHMEN COMING TO MARS.

NORMAN THOUGHT IT WAS A WONDERFUL STORY AND SUGGESTED THAT I WRITE MORE OF THESE, SO OVER THE NEXT FEW YEARS I WROTE OVER A DOZEN MARTIAN STORIES, LITTLE REALIZING I WAS WRITING A NOVEL.

AT THE SAME TIME, I READ *THE GRAPES OF WRATH*, BY JOHN STEINBECK. STEINBECK WAS TEACHING ME HOW TO WRITE NOT ONLY ORDINARY CHAPTERS BUT PROSE POEMS.

DURING THAT SAME PERIOD MY WIFE, MAGGIE, GOT PREGNANT. HAVING LITTLE MONEY, I DECIDED TO TRY AND GET TO NEW YORK TO SEE IF I COULD SELL MY STORIES.

I MET MANY EDITORS ON THAT TRIP, BUT NONE OF THEM WANTED ANYTHING TO DO WITH ME BECAUSE I WAS A SHORT STORY WRITER AND NOT A NOVELIST.

ON MY LAST NIGHT IN NEW YORK I HAD DINNER WITH WALTER BRADBURY--NO RELATION--OF DOUBLEDAY, AND HE SAID TO ME, "RAY, I THINK YOU'VE WRITTEN A NOVEL BUT YOU DON'T KNOW IT."

I SAID, "WHAT HAVE I DONE?"

HE SAID, "ALL THOSE MARTIAN STORIES THAT YOU'VE PUBLISHED, WHAT IF YOU PUT THEM TOGETHER AND MADE A TAPESTRY OF THEM AND WE'D CALL IT *THE MARTIAN CHRONICLES*."

I SAID, "THAT'S A GOOD TITLE, CAN I BORROW THAT?"

HE SAID, "YES, IT'S YOURS."

HE THEN TOLD ME, "GO BACK TO THE YMCA AND TYPE AN OUTLINE OF THIS TAPESTRY OF STORIES YOU'VE WRITTEN AND BRING IT TO ME TOMORROW. IF IT'S ANY GOOD I'LL GIVE YOU AN ADVANCE OF $700."

I WENT BACK TO THE YMCA--THE ONLY PLACE I COULD AFFORD--STAYED UP ALL NIGHT AND TYPED AN OUTLINE FOR THIS BOOK. I BROUGHT IT TO WALTER BRADBURY THE NEXT DAY AND HE SAID:

"MY GOD, THAT'S IT! YOU'VE WRITTEN A BOOK ABOUT MARS. EVERYTHING IS INTUITION WITH YOU AND THIS IS PURE POETRY. NOW GO HOME AND FINISH THE BOOK."

I WENT BACK TO MY PREGNANT WIFE IN VENICE, CALIFORNIA, AND OVER THE NEXT SEVERAL MONTHS I FILLED IN ALL THE CORNERS AND CREVICES OF THIS BOOK ABOUT MARS AND FINALLY SENT IT TO DOUBLEDAY, WHO PUBLISHED IT IN THE SPRING OF 1950.

THERE WERE NO REVIEWS OF THAT BOOK; NOBODY REALLY CARED THAT I WROTE BOOKS, ESPECIALLY ABOUT MARS. BUT ONE DAY I WENT INTO A BOOKSTORE AND BUMPED INTO CHRISTOPHER ISHERWOOD, THE ENGLISH AUTHOR, AND GAVE HIM A COPY OF MY BOOK.

HIS FACE FELL AND I COULD SEE THAT HE DIDN'T WANT TO READ THE DARNED THING, BUT THREE DAYS LATER HE CALLED ME AND SAID, "RAY, DO YOU KNOW WHAT YOU'VE DONE?"

I SAID, "WHAT?"

HE SAID, "YOU'VE WRITTEN AN EXTRAORDINARY BOOK ABOUT MARS AND I'M GOING TO REVIEW IT FOR *TOMORROW MAGAZINE*."

HE DID THAT REVIEW, WHICH WAS WONDERFUL, AND THEN CALLED AND SAID, "ALDOUS HUXLEY WANTS TO MEET YOU FOR TEA."

I TOLD HIM, "I'LL GO TO SEE MR. HUXLEY. I WON'T HAVE TEA, BUT I'LL TALK WITH HIM."

WHEN I GOT TO MR. HUXLEY'S HOUSE HE SAID TO ME, "MR. BRADBURY, DO YOU KNOW WHAT YOU ARE?"

I SAID, "WHAT AM I?"

"YOU ARE A POET," HE SAID. "YOU ARE A POET. YOU HAVE WRITTEN A BOOK OF POETRY ABOUT MARS. IT'S MORE THAN JUST FICTION, IT'S MORE THAN JUST WORDS, IT'S MAGICAL WORDS. YOU'VE MADE MARS A REAL PLACE AND WE'RE ALL GOING TO TRAVEL THERE AND WE'RE NOT GOING TO COME BACK, ALL BECAUSE OF YOU. YOU GOT THERE FIRST, WERE THE FIRST MARTIAN. THANK YOU FOR THAT BOOK."

SO HERE IT ALL IS: MY LIVING ON LOWELL AVENUE WHEN I WAS SIX, MY FALLING IN LOVE WITH JOHN CARTER AND MARS WHEN I WAS TWELVE, AND MEETING ALL THESE OTHER WONDERFUL PEOPLE IN MY TWENTIES AND WRITING THESE STORIES. HERE THEY ALL ARE, IN WHAT APPEARS TO BE A NOVEL. I INVITE YOU TO COME TO MARS WITH ME AND STAY FOREVER.

RAY BRADBURY
JUNE 2011

RAY BRADBURY'S

THE MARTIAN CHRONICLES

ONE MINUTE IT WAS OHIO WINTER, WITH DOORS CLOSED, WINDOWS LOCKED, THE PANES BLIND WITH FROST, ICICLES FRINGING EVERY ROOF, CHILDREN SKIING ON SLOPES, HOUSEWIVES LUMBERING LIKE GREAT BLACK BEARS IN THEIR FURS ALONG THE ICY STREETS.

AND THEN A LONG WAVE OF WARMTH CROSSED THE SMALL TOWN. A FLOODING SEA OF HOT AIR; IT SEEMED AS IF SOMEONE HAD LEFT A BAKERY DOOR OPEN. THE HEAT PULSED AMONG THE COTTAGES AND BUSHES AND CHILDREN. THE ICICLES DROPPED, SHATTERING, TO MELT. THE DOORS FLEW OPEN. THE WIDOWS FLEW UP.

THE CHILDREN WORKED OFF THEIR WOOL CLOTHES. THE HOUSEWIVES SHED THEIR BEAR DISGUISES. THE SNOW DISSOLVED AND SHOWED LAST SUMMER'S ANCIENT GREEN LAWNS.

ROCKET SUMMER. PEOPLE LEANED FROM THEIR DRIPPING PORCHES AND WATCHED THE REDDENING SKY.

ROCKET SUMMER. THE WORDS PASSED AMONG THE PEOPLE IN THE OPEN, AIRING HOUSES. ROCKET SUMMER. THE WARM DESERT AIR CHANGING THE FROST PATTERNS ON THE WINDOWS, ERASING THE ART WORK. THE SKIS AND SLEDS SUDDENLY USELESS. THE SNOW, FALLING FROM THE COLD SKY UPON THE TOWN, TURNED TO A HOT RAIN BEFORE IT TOUCHED THE GROUND.

THE ROCKET LAY ON THE LAUNCHING FIELD, BLOWING OUT PINK CLOUDS OF FIRE AND OVEN HEAT. THE ROCKET STOOD IN THE COLD WINTER MORNING, MAKING SUMMER WITH EVERY BREATH OF ITS MIGHTY EXHAUSTS. THE ROCKET MADE CLIMATES, AND SUMMER LAY FOR A BRIEF MOMENT UPON THE LAND.

5

6

YOU'VE BEEN DREAMING AGAIN! YOU SPOKE OUT AND KEPT ME AWAKE. I REALLY THINK YOU SHOULD SEE A DOCTOR.

I'LL BE ALL RIGHT.

YOU TALKED A LOT IN YOUR SLEEP!

DID I?

WHAT WAS YOUR DREAM?

THE SHIP. IT CAME FROM THE SKY AGAIN, LANDED.

THE TALL MAN STEPPED OUT AND TALKED TO ME, TELLING ME LITTLE JOKES, LAUGHING, AND IT WAS PLEASANT.

AND THEN, THIS MAN, WHO SAID HIS STRANGE NAME WAS NATHANIEL YORK, TOLD ME I WAS BEAUTIFUL AND--

--AND KISSED ME.

13

HALF AN HOUR LATER, MR. AAA, SEATED IN HIS LIBRARY SIPPING A BIT OF ELECTRIC FIRE FROM A METAL CUP, HEARD THE VOICES OUTSIDE IN THE STONE CAUSEWAY.

ARE YOU MR. AAA?

I AM.

MR. TTT SENT US TO SEE YOU!

WHY DID HE DO THAT?

HE WAS BUSY!

DOES HE THINK I HAVE NOTHING ELSE TO DO BUT ENTERTAIN PEOPLE HE'S TOO BUSY TO BOTHER WITH?

THAT'S NOT THE IMPORTANT THING, SIR!

WELL, IT IS TO ME. I HAVE MUCH READING TO DO.

NOW, DO YOU THINK IT FAIR OF MR. TTT TO BE SO ILL-MANNERED?

WE'RE FROM EARTH!

I THINK IT VERY UNGENTLEMANLY OF HIM.

A ROCKET SHIP, WE CAME IN IT. OVER THERE!

JUST THE FOUR OF US; MYSELF AND THESE THREE MEN, MY CREW.

I'LL CALL HIM UP, YES, THAT'S WHAT I'LL DO!

CHALLENGED HIM TO A DUEL, BY THE GODS! A DUEL!

MR. AAA--

I'LL SHOOT HIM DEAD, DO YOU HEAR!

MR. AAA...WE CAME SIXTY MILLION MILES.

WHERE'D YOU SAY YOU WERE FROM?

FROM EARTH!

THAT'S ONLY FIFTY MILLION MILES THIS TIME OF YEAR.

WELL, I HAVE TO GO NOW.

JUST TAKE THAT SILLY NOTE INTO THE LITTLE TOWN OF IOPR AND TELL MR. III ALL ABOUT IT. HE'S THE MAN YOU WANT TO SEE.

NOT MR. TTT, HE'S AN IDIOT. I'M GOING TO KILL HIM. NOT ME--BECAUSE YOU'RE NOT IN MY LINE OF WORK.

DO YOU HAVE TO BE IN A CERTAIN LINE OF WORK TO WELCOME EARTH MEN!

DON'T BE SILLY, EVERYONE KNOWS THAT! GOOD-BY!

27

THE FOUR BODIES LAY IN THE SUN.

A SHOT RANG OUT. MR. XXX LAY WHERE HE FELL.

WHEN THE TOWN PEOPLE FOUND THE ROCKET, THEY WONDERED WHAT IT WAS. NOBODY KNEW. IT WAS SOLD TO A JUNKMAN AND HAULED OFF FOR SCRAP METAL.

34

35

IT'S NOT EVERY DAY YOU GET A SECOND CHANCE TO LIVE.

I'LL WAKE IN THE MORNING. AND I'LL BE IN THE ROCKET, IN SPACE, AND ALL THIS WILL BE GONE.

"DON'T THINK THAT. DON'T QUESTION. GOD'S GOOD TO US. LET'S BE HAPPY."

SORRY, MOM.

YOU'RE TIRED, SON. YOUR OLD BEDROOM'S WAITING FOR YOU, BRASS BED AND ALL.

BUT I SHOULD REPORT MY MEN IN.

WHY?

WHY? WELL, I DON'T KNOW.

THEY'RE ALL EATING OR IN BED. A GOOD NIGHT'S SLEEP WON'T HURT THEM.

GOOD NIGHT, SON. IT'S GOOD TO HAVE YOU HOME.

IT'S GOOD TO BE HOME.

37

HE HAD THE MOST RIDICULOUS THEORY QUITE SUDDENLY. IT GAVE HIM KIND OF A CHILL. IT WAS REALLY NOTHING TO CONSIDER, OF COURSE. HIGHLY IMPROBABLE.

SILLY.

FORGET IT.

RIDICULOUS.

BUT JUST SUPPOSE...

...THAT THERE WERE MARTIANS AND THEY SAW OUR SHIP COMING AND SAW US INSIDE OUR SHIP AND HATED US.

SUPPOSE THEY WANTED TO DESTROY US, AS INVADERS, AND THEY WANTED TO DO IT IN A VERY CLEVER WAY...

TELEPATHY, HYPNOSIS, MEMORY, AND IMAGINATION.

SUPPOSE ALL OF THESE HOUSES AREN'T REAL AT ALL, THIS BED NOT REAL, BUT ONLY FIGMENTS OF MY OWN IMAGINATION...

...GIVEN SUBSTANCE BY TELEPATHY AND HYPNOSIS THROUGH THE MARTIANS.

WHAT BETTER WAY TO FOOL A MAN, USING HIS OWN MOTHER AND FATHER AS BAIT?

WHAT IF THE MARTIANS TOOK THE MEMORIES OF A TOWN FROM MY MIND?

AND AFTER THEY BUILT THE TOWN, THEY POPULATED IT WITH THE MOST-LOVED PEOPLE FROM ALL THE MINDS OF THE PEOPLE ON THE ROCKET!

AND SUPPOSE THOSE TWO PEOPLE IN THE NEXT ROOM ARE NOT MY MOTHER AND FATHER AT ALL, BUT TWO MARTIANS...

WITH THE ABILITY TO KEEP ME UNDER THIS DREAMING HYPNOSIS ALL OF THE TIME.

ALL OF THIS...PART OF SOME GREAT CLEVER PLAN TO DIVIDE AND CON-QUER US, AND KILL US?

PERHAPS MY BROTHER WILL CHANGE FORM, MELT, SHIFT, AND BECOME ANOTHER THING...IT WOULD BE SIMPLE FOR HIM TO TURN OVER AND PUT A KNIFE INTO MY HEART.

IN THE MORNING...ALONG THE SUN-FILLED STREET, WEEPING, CAME THE GRANDMAS AND MOTHERS AND SISTERS AND THE CHURCHYARD...

WHERE THERE WERE NEW HOLES FRESHLY DUG...

...SIXTEEN HOLES IN ALL.

THE MAYOR MADE A LITTLE SAD SPEECH, HIS FACE SOMETIMES LOOKING LIKE THE MAYOR, SOMETIMES LOOKING LIKE SOMETHING ELSE...

MOTHER AND FATHER BLACK WERE THERE... THEIR FACES MELTING NOW... ...SHIFTING LIKE WAX.

THE COFFINS WERE LOWERED...

EARTH POUNDED DOWN ON THE COFFIN LIDS.

THE BRASS BAND MARCHED BACK INTO TOWN, AND EVERYONE TOOK THE DAY OFF.

41

43

45

47

THEY WERE ALL WHISPERING NOW, FOR IT WAS LIKE ENTERING A VAST OPEN LIBRARY OR A MAUSOLEUM IN WHICH THE WIND LIVED AND OVER WHICH THE STARS SHONE...

THE CAPTAIN WONDERED WHERE THE PEOPLE HAD GONE, AND WHAT THEY HAD BEEN, AND WHO THEIR KINGS WERE, AND HOW THEY HAD DIED.

AND HE WONDERED HOW THEY HAD BUILT THIS CITY TO LAST THE AGES THROUGH, AND HAD THEY EVER COME TO EARTH? WERE THEY ANCESTORS OF EARTH MEN TEN THOUSAND YEARS REMOVED?

LORD BYRON.

LORD WHO?

LORD BYRON, A NINETEENTH-CENTURY POET.

HE WROTE A POEM A LONG TIME AGO THAT FITS THIS CITY AND HOW THE MARTIANS MUST FEEL, IF THERE'S ANYTHING LEFT OF THEM TO FEEL. IT MIGHT HAVE BEEN WRITTEN BY THE LAST MARTIAN POET.

HOW DOES THE POEM GO, SPENDER?

49

SO WE'LL GO NO MORE
A-ROVING

SO LATE INTO THE NIGHT,

THOUGH THE HEART BE
STILL AS LOVING,

AND THE MOON BE
STILL AS BRIGHT...

FOR THE SWORD OUT-
WEARS ITS SHEATH,

AND THE SOUL WEARS
OUT THE BREAST,

AND THE HEART MUST
PAUSE TO BREATHE,

AND LOVE ITSELF
MUST REST.

THOUGH THE NIGHT WAS
MADE FOR LOVING,

AND THE DAY RETURNS
TOO SOON,

YET WE'LL GO NO MORE
A-ROVING

BY THE LIGHT OF
THE MOON.

WITHOUT A WORD,
THE EARTH MEN STOOD IN
THE CENTER OF THE CITY.

BIGGS MADE A
SICK NOISE
IN HIS
THROAT.

NO ONE
MOVED TO
HELP BIGGS.

SPENDER STOOD FOR A MOMENT,
THEN TURNED AND WALKED OFF...
ALONE IN THE MOONLIGHT.

53

...UP IN A DEAD TOWN. I DIDN'T THINK I'D FIND HIM.

I'VE BEEN LIVING IN A LITTLE VALLEY TOWN FOR ABOUT A WEEK, LEARNING HOW TO READ THE ANCIENT BOOKS AND LOOKING AT THEIR OLD ART FORMS...

...ON THE DAY I LEARNED HOW TO DECIPHER THE MARTIAN LANGUAGE--IT'S AMAZINGLY SIMPLE--THE MARTIAN APPEARED BEFORE ME AND SAID, "GIVE ME YOUR BOOTS."

HE SAID, "GIVE ME YOUR UNIFORM AND ALL THE REST OF YOUR APPAREL."

THEN HE SAID, "GIVE ME YOUR GUN...NOW COME ALONG AND WATCH WHAT HAPPENS."

AND THE MARTIAN WALKED DOWN INTO CAMP AND HE'S HERE NOW.

I DON'T SEE ANY MARTIAN.

I'M SORRY.

55

SPENDER SAW THE THIN
DUST RISING IN SEVERAL
PLACES IN THE VALLEY...

...HE KNEW THE PURSUIT
WAS ORGANIZED
AND READY.

THE FIRING BEGAN
ABOUT THREE IN
THE AFTERNOON.

WITH HIS FIRST SHOT, HE DROPPED ONE
OF THE MEN DEAD IN HIS TRACKS.

SUDDENLY THE CAPTAIN STOOD UP.

HE CAME WALKING UP THE MOUNTAIN
AND SAT ON A WARM BOULDER.

60

YOU'VE GOT IT ALL PLANNED. YET YOU'RE OUTNUMBERED. IN AN HOUR WE'LL HAVE YOU SURROUNDED. IN AN HOUR YOU'LL BE DEAD.

I'VE FOUND SOME UNDER-GROUND PASSAGES YOU'LL NEVER FIND. I'LL WITHDRAW THERE TO LIVE FOR A FEW WEEKS. UNTIL YOU'RE OFF GUARD. I'LL COME OUT THEN TO PICK YOU OFF, ONE BY ONE.

TELL ME ABOUT YOUR CIVILIZATION HERE.

THEY KNEW HOW TO LIVE WITH NATURE AND GET ALONG WITH NATURE. THEY DIDN'T TRY TOO HARD TO BE ALL MEN AND NO ANIMAL.

THEY KNEW HOW TO COMBINE SCIENCE AND RELIGION SO THE TWO WORKED SIDE BY SIDE, NEITHER DENYING THE OTHER, EACH ENRICHING THE OTHER.

THAT SOUNDS IDEAL.

IT WAS. I'D LIKE TO SHOW YOU HOW THE MARTIANS DID IT.

MY MEN ARE WAITING.

WE'LL BE GONE HALF AN HOUR. TELL THEM THAT, SIR.

THERE'S YOUR ANSWER, CAPTAIN.

I DON'T SEE.

61

THE MEN RAN AND DUCKED AND RAN AND SQUATTED IN SHADOWS...

SPENDER REMAINED WHERE HE WAS, FIRING ONLY ON OCCASION.

HEY, YOU! HERE'S A SLUG FOR YOUR HEAD!

GO ON, SPENDER... GET OUT...YOU'VE ONLY GOT A FEW MINUTES TO ESCAPE.

SPENDER DID NOT MOVE FROM HIS POSITION.

WAS IT BECAUSE OF ME? AM I ANY DIFFERENT FROM THESE OTHERS HERE? DID HE FIGURE HE COULD TRUST ME?

HE'S DEAD.

I'VE GOT TO LIVE UP TO THIS. IF HE FIGURED THERE WAS SOMETHING IN ME THAT WAS LIKE HIMSELF AND COULDN'T KILL ME BECAUSE OF IT, THEN WHAT A JOB I HAVE AHEAD OF ME!

I GUESS YOU'RE RIGHT. WE COULD NEVER HAVE GOT TOGETHER. SPENDER AND *MYSELF*, PERHAPS...

IF ONLY HE HAD COME TO ME AND TALKED IT OVER BEFORE HE SHOT ANYBODY, WE COULD HAVE WORKED IT OUT SOMEHOW.

WORKED WHAT OUT? WHAT COULD WE HAVE WORKED OUT WITH HIS LIKES?

THE NEXT AFTERNOON PARKHILL DID TARGET PRACTICE IN ONE OF THE DEAD CITIES, SHOOTING OUT CRYSTAL WINDOWS AND BLOWING THE TOPS OFF FRAGILE TOWERS. THE CAPTAIN CAUGHT PARKHILL AND KNOCKED HIS TEETH OUT.

BUT SPENDER AND YOU AND THE OTHERS, NO, NEVER. HE'S BETTER OFF NOW.

67

HIS NAME WAS BENJAMIN DRISCOLL, AND HE WAS THIRTY-ONE YEARS OLD. AND THE THING THAT HE WANTED WAS MARS GROWN GREEN AND TALL WITH TREES AND FOLIAGE, PRODUCING AIR, MORE AIR, GROWING LARGER WITH EACH SEASON...

TREES TO COOL THE TOWNS IN THE BOILING SUMMER, TREES TO HOLD BACK THE WINTER WINDS.

THERE WERE SO MANY THINGS A TREE COULD DO...ADD COLOR, PROVIDE SHADE, DROP FRUIT, OR BECOME A CHIDREN'S PLAYGROUND, A WHOLE SKY UNIVERSE TO CLIMB AND HANG FROM; AN ARCHITECTURE OF FOOD AND PLEASURE...

...THAT WAS A TREE.

BUT MOST OF ALL THE TREES WOULD DISTILL AN ICY AIR FOR THE LUNGS, AND A GENTLE RUSTLING FOR THE EAR WHEN YOU LAY NIGHTS IN YOUR SNOWY BED AND WERE GENTLED TO SLEEP BY THE SOUND

HE LAY LISTENING TO THE DARK EARTH GATHER ITSELF, WAITING FOR THE SUN, FOR THE RAINS THAT HADN'T COME YET.

BUT YOU'LL LET ME DO IT?

THEY LET HIM DO IT. PROVIDED WITH A SINGLE MOTORCYCLE, ITS BIN FULL OF RICH SEEDS AND SPROUTS, HE HAD PARKED HIS VEHICLE IN THE VALLEY WILDERNESS AND STRUCK OUT ON FOOT OVER THE LAND.

HE KEPT HIS EYES ONLY AHEAD OF HIM, WAITING FOR THE RAINS TO COME.

HE AND THE CO-ORDINATOR HAD TALKED AN ENTIRE MORNING ABOUT THINGS THAT GREW AND WERE GREEN. IT WOULD BE MONTHS, IF NOT YEARS, BEFORE ORGANIZED PLANTING BEGAN. SO FAR, FROSTED FOOD WAS BROUGHT FROM EARTH IN FLYING ICICLES...A FEW COMMUNITY GARDENS WERE GREENING UP IN HYDROPONIC PLANTS.

THAT HAD BEEN THIRTY DAYS AGO, AND HE HAD NEVER GLANCED BACK. THE WEATHER WAS EXCESSIVELY DRY; IT WAS DOUBTFUL IF ANY SEEDS HAD SPROUTED YET.

THE FIRE FLUTTERED INTO SLEEPY ASH. THE AIR TREMORED TO THE DISTANT ROLL OF A CARTWHEEL. THUNDER. A SUDDEN ODOR OF WATER. TONIGHT, HE THOUGHT, AND PUT HIS HAND OUT TO FEEL FOR RAIN. TONIGHT.

IT RAINED STEADILY FOR TWO HOURS AND THEN STOPPED. THE STARS CAME OUT, FRESHLY WASHED AND CLEARER THAN EVER.

HE WAITED A MOMENT BEFORE ARISING. HE HAD WORKED AND WAITED A LONG HOT MONTH, AND NOW, STANDING UP, HE TURNED AT LAST AND FACED THE DIRECTION FROM WHICH HE HAD COME.

IT WAS A GREEN MORNING.

NOT ONE TREE, NOT TWO, NOT A DOZEN, BUT THE THOUSANDS HE HAD PLANTED IN SEED AND SPROUT.

AND NOT LITTLE TREES, NO, NOT SAPLINGS, NOT LITTLE TENDER SHOOTS, BUT GREAT TREES, HUGE TREES, TREES AS TALL AS TEN MEN, GREEN AND GREEN AND HUGE AND ROUND AND FULL, TREES SHIMMERING THEIR METALLIC LEAVES, TREES WHISPERING, TREES IN A LINE OVER HILLS.

IMPOSSIBLE!

LEMON TREES, LIME TREES, REDWOODS AND MIMOSAS AND OAKS AND ELMS AND ASPENS, CHERRY, MAPLE, ASH, APPLE, ORANGE, EUCALYPTUS, STUNG BY A TUMULTUOUS RAIN, NOURISHED BY ALIEN AND MAGICAL SOIL AND, EVEN AS HE WATCHED, THROWING OUT NEW BRANCHES, POPPING OPEN NEW BUDS.

THE VALLEY AND THE MORNING WERE GREEN. AND THE AIR!

ALL ABOUT, LIKE A MOVING CURRENT, A MOUNTAIN RIVER, CAME THE NEW AIR, THE OXYGEN BLOWING FROM THE GREEN TREES. YOU COULD SEE IT SHIMMER HIGH IN CRYSTAL BILLOWS. OXYGEN, FRESH, PURE, GREEN, COLD OXYGEN TURNING THE VALLEY INTO A RIVER DELTA.

MR. BENJAMIN DRISCOLL TOOK ONE LONG DEEP DRINK OF GREEN WATER AIR AND FAINTED.

BEFORE HE WOKE AGAIN FIVE THOUSAND NEW TREES HAD CLIMBED UP INTO THE YELLOW SUN.

71

73

75

WE BROUGHT IN A MILLION BOARD FEET OF OREGON LUMBER AND A COUPLE DOZEN TONS OF GOOD STEEL NAILS AND HAMMERED TOGETHER TWO OF THE NICEST LITTLE VILLAGES YOU EVER SAW.

TONIGHT WE'RE WARMING ONE OF THEM. A COUPLE ROCKETS ARE COMING IN FROM EARTH, BRINGING OUR WIVES AND GIRL FRIENDS. THERE'LL BE BARN DANCES AND WHISKY—

OH, YOU'RE QUITE WRONG. SEE ALL THE CARNIVAL LIGHTS? THERE ARE BEAUTIFUL BOATS AS SLIM AS WOMEN, BEAUTIFUL WOMEN AS SLIM AS BOATS, WOMEN THE COLOR OF SAND, WOMEN WITH FIRE FLOWERS IN THEIR HANDS.

MISTER, THAT CITY IS DEAD AS A DRIED LIZARD. ASK ANY OF OUR PARTY.

ME, I'M ON MY WAY TO GREEN CITY TONIGHT; THAT'S THE NEW COLONY WE JUST RAISED OVER NEAR ILLINOIS HIGHWAY. YOU'RE MIXED UP.

YOU SAY IT'S OVER *THAT* WAY?

THAT'S WHERE I'M GOING NOW, TO THE FESTIVAL; WE'LL FLOAT ON THE WATERS ALL NIGHT LONG; WE'LL SING, WE'LL DRINK, WE'LL MAKE LOVE. CAN'T YOU SEE IT?

76

79

THEY BROUGHT IN FIFTEEN THOUSAND LUMBER FEET OF OREGON PINE TO BUILD TENTH CITY, AND SEVENTY-NINE THOUSAND FEET OF CALIFORNIA REDWOOD AND THEY HAMMERED TOGETHER A CLEAN, NEAT LITTLE TOWN BY THE EDGE OF THE STONE CANALS.

ON SUNDAY NIGHTS YOU COULD SEE RED, BLUE, AND GREEN STAINED-GLASS LIGHT IN THE CHURCHES AND HEAR THE VOICES SINGING THE NUMBERED HYMNS.

AND IN CERTAIN HOUSES YOU HEARD THE HARD CLATTER OF A TYPEWRITER, THE NOVELIST AT WORK; OR THE SCRATCH OF A PEN, THE POET AT WORK; OR NO SOUND AT ALL, THE FORMER BEACHCOMBER AT WORK.

"WE WILL NOW SING 79. WE WILL NOW SING 94."

IT WAS AS IF, IN MANY WAYS, A GREAT EARTH-QUAKE HAD SHAKEN LOOSE THE ROOTS AND CELLARS OF AN IOWA TOWN, AND THEN, IN AN INSTANT, A WHIRLWIND TWISTER OF OZ-LIKE PROPORTIONS HAD CARRIED THE ENTIRE TOWN OFF TO MARS TO SET IT DOWN WITHOUT A BUMP.

THE BOYS WOULD HIKE FAR OUT INTO THE MARTIAN COUNTRY.

FIRST ONE THERE GETS TO KICK.

THEY CARRIED ODOROUS PAPER BAGS INTO WHICH FROM TIME TO TIME UPON THE LONG WALK THEY WOULD INSERT THEIR NOSES TO INHALE THE RICH SMELL OF THE HAM AND MAYONNAISED PICKLES, AND TO LISTEN TO THE LIQUID GURGLE OF THE ORANGE SODA IN THE WARMING BOTTLES. THEY WOULD DARE EACH OTHER ON PAST THE LIMITS SET BY THEIR STERN MOTHERS.

THEY WOULD RUN, YELLING:

81

THEY HIKED IN SUMMER, AUTUMN, OR WINTER. AUTUMN WAS MOST FUN, BECAUSE THEN THEY IMAGINED, LIKE ON EARTH, THEY WERE SCUTTERING THROUGH AUTUMN LEAVES.

THEY WOULD COME LIKE A SCATTER OF JACK-STONES ON THE MARBLE FLATS BESIDE THE CANALS, THE CANDY-CHEEKED BOYS WITH BLUE-AGATE EYES, PANTING ONION-TAINTED COMMANDS TO EACH OTHER. FOR NOW THAT THEY HAD REACHED THE DEAD, FORBIDDEN TOWN IT WAS NO LONGER A MATTER OF "LAST ONE THERE'S A GIRL!" OR "FIRST ONE GETS TO PLAY MUSICIAN!"

NOW THE DEAD TOWN'S DOORS LAY WIDE AND THEY THOUGHT THEY COULD HEAR THE FAINTEST CRACKLE, LIKE AUTUMN LEAVES, FROM INSIDE. THEY WOULD HUSH THEMSELVES FORWARD, REMEMBERING THEIR PARENTS HAD TOLD THEM...

NOT THERE! NO, TO NONE OF THE OLD TOWNS! WATCH WHERE YOU HIKE. YOU'LL GET THE BEATING OF YOUR LIFE WHEN YOU COME HOME. WE'LL CHECK YOUR SHOES!!

HERE GOES NOTHING!

AND THERE THEY STOOD IN THE DEAD CITY, A HEAP OF BOYS, THEIR HIKING LUNCHES HALF DEVOURED, DARING EACH OTHER IN SHRIEKY WHISPERS.

AND THEN OUT OF ONE HOUSE INTO ANOTHER, INTO SEVENTEEN HOUSES, MINDFUL THAT EACH OF THE TOWNS IN ITS TURN WAS BEING BURNED CLEAN OF ITS HORRORS BY THE FIREMEN, ANTISEPTIC WARRIORS WITH SHOVELS AND BINS.

SHOVELING AWAY AT THE EBONY TATTERS AND PEPPERMINT-STICK BONES, SLOWLY BUT ASSUREDLY SEPARATING THE TERRIBLE FROM THE NORMAL; SO THEY MUST PLAY VERY HARD,THESE BOYS, THE FIREMEN WOULD SOON BE HERE!

THEN, LUMINOUS WITH SWEAT, THEY GNASHED AT THEIR LAST SANDWICHES. WITH A FINAL KICK, A FINAL MARIMBA CONCERT, A FINAL AUTUMNAL LUNGE THROUGH LEAF STACKS, THEY WENT HOME.

THEIR MOTHERS EXAMINED THEIR SHOES FOR BLACK FLAKELETS WHICH, WHEN DISCOVERED, RESULTED IN SCALDING BATHS AND FATHERLY BEATINGS.

BY THE YEAR'S END THE FIREMEN HAD RAKED THE AUTUMN LEAVES AND WHITE XYLOPHONES AWAY, AND IT WAS NO MORE FUN.

85

87

93

94

95

97

99

101

103

105

YOU'RE NOT SAFE IN THE TOWN. IT'S BETTER OUT ON THE CANAL WHERE NO ONE CAN HURT YOU.

THAT'S TRUE...

BUT I MUST CONSIDER THESE PEOPLE NOW. HOW WOULD THEY FEEL IF, IN THE MORNING, I WAS GONE AGAIN, THIS TIME FOR GOOD?

ANYWAY, THE MOTHER KNOWS WHAT I AM; SHE GUESSED, EVEN AS YOU DID. I THINK THEY ALL GUESSED BUT DIDN'T QUESTION. YOU DON'T QUESTION PROVIDENCE.

IF YOU CAN'T HAVE THE REALITY, A DREAM IS JUST AS GOOD. PERHAPS I'M NOT THEIR DEAD ONE BACK, BUT I'M SOMETHING ALMOST BETTER TO THEM; AN IDEAL SHAPED BY THEIR MINDS. I HAVE A CHOICE OF HURTING THEM OR YOUR WIFE.

THEY'RE A FAMILY OF FIVE. THEY CAN STAND YOUR LOSS BETTER!

PLEASE. I'M TIRED.

107

HE PULLED THE
DOOR WIDE AND
LOOKED OUT.

...HE SHUT AND
BOLTED THE DOOR.

HE WAITED FIVE
MINUTES AND
THEN SOFTLY...

124

SAM, STOP THE SHIP.

NO, YOU DON'T. NOT AFTER ALL THIS TIME, *YOU'RE NOT PULLING OUT ON ME.*

I BELIEVE YOU WOULD. YOU ACTUALLY WOULD.

ELMA, THIS IS CRAZY. WE'LL BE IN TOWN IN A MINUTE, WE'LL BE OKAY!

ELMA, LISTEN TO ME.

THERE'S NOTHING TO HEAR, SAM.

ELMA!

125

129

THEY ALL CAME OUT AND LOOKED AT THE SKY THAT NIGHT.

THEY LEFT THEIR SUPPERS OR THEIR WASHING UP OR THEIR DRESSING FOR THE SHOW AND THEY CAME OUT UPON THEIR NOW-NOT-QUITE-AS-NEW PORCHES AND WATCHED THE GREEN STAR OF EARTH THERE.

IT WAS A MOVE WITHOUT CONSCIOUS EFFORT; THEY ALL DID IT, TO HELP THEM UNDERSTAND THE NEWS THEY HAD HEARD ON THE RADIO A MOMENT BEFORE.

HERE WAS EARTH AND THERE THE COMING WAR, AND THERE HUNDREDS OF THOUSANDS OF MOTHERS OR GRANDMOTHERS OR FATHERS OR BROTHERS OR AUNTS OR UNCLES OR COUSINS. THEY STOOD ON THE PORCHES AND TRIED TO BELIEVE IN THE EXISTENCE OF EARTH, MUCH AS THEY HAD ONCE TRIED TO BELIEVE IN THE EXISTENCE OF MARS; IT WAS A PROBLEM REVERSED.

TO ALL INTENTS AND PURPOSES, EARTH NOW WAS DEAD.

AT NINE O'CLOCK EARTH SEEMED TO EXPLODE, CATCH FIRE, AND BURN.

BUT NOBODY MOVED. LATE DINNERS WERE CARRIED OUT ONTO THE NIGHT LAWNS AND SET UPON COLLAPSIBLE TABLES.

AND THEY PICKED AT THESE SLOWLY UNTIL TWO O'CLOCK AND THE LIGHT-RADIO MESSAGE FLASHED FROM EARTH.

THEY COULD READ THE GREAT MORSE-CODE FLASHES WHICH FLICKERED LIKE A DISTANT FIREFLY:

AUSTRALIAN CONTINENT ATOMIZED IN PREMATURE EXPLOSION OF ATOMIC STOCKPILE.

LOS ANGELES, LONDON BOMBED. WAR. COME HOME. COME HOME.

COME HOME.

135

SOMEHOW THE IDEA WAS BROUGHT UP BY MOM THAT PERHAPS THE WHOLE FAMILY WOULD ENJOY A FISHING TRIP.

BUT THEY WEREN'T MOM'S WORDS. TIMOTHY KNEW THAT. THEY WERE DAD'S WORDS, AND MOM USED THEM FOR HIM SOMEHOW.

LOOK, KIDS...

THERE'S A DEAD CITY.

TIMOTHY LOOKED AT THE DEEP OCEAN SKY, TRYING TO SEE EARTH AND THE WAR AND THE RUINED CITIES AND THE MEN KILLING EACH OTHER SINCE THE DAY HE WAS BORN. BUT HE SAW NOTHING.

THE WAR WAS AS REMOVED AND FAR OFF AS TWO FLIES BATTLING TO THE DEATH IN THE ARCH OF A GREAT HIGH AND SILENT CATHEDRAL.

I THOUGHT IT WAS A ROCKET.

AND JUST AS SENSELESS.

139

143

146

147

THEY STOOD THERE, KING OF THE HILL, TOP OF THE HEAP, RULER OF ALL THEY SURVEYED, UNIMPEACHABLE MONARCHS AND PRESIDENTS, TRYING TO UNDERSTAND WHAT IT MEANT TO OWN A WORLD AND HOW BIG A WORLD REALLY WAS.

IT'S TIME I TOLD YOU A FEW THINGS.

I DON'T SUPPOSE IT WAS FAIR, KEEPING SO MUCH FROM YOU. I DON'T KNOW IF YOU'LL UNDERSTAND, BUT I HAVE TO TALK, EVEN IF ONLY PART OF IT GETS OVER TO YOU.

WE WERE LUCKY. THERE AREN'T ANY MORE ROCKETS LEFT. IT'S TIME YOU KNEW...EARTH IS GONE.

I'M BURNING A WAY OF LIFE, JUST LIKE THAT WAY OF LIFE IS BEING BURNED CLEAN OF EARTH RIGHT NOW. FORGIVE ME IF I TALK LIKE A POLITICIAN. I AM, AFTER ALL, A FORMER STATE GOVERNOR, AND I WAS HONEST AND THEY HATED ME FOR IT.

INTERPLANETARY TRAVEL WON'T BE BACK FOR CENTURIES, MAYBE NEVER. BUT THAT WAY OF LIFE PROVED ITSELF WRONG AND STRANGLED ITSELF WITH ITS OWN HANDS.

SCIENCE RAN TOO FAR AHEAD OF US TOO QUICKLY, AND THE PEOPLE GOT LOST IN A MECHANICAL WILDERNESS, LIKE CHILDREN... EMPHASIZING THE WRONG ITEMS, EMPHASIZING MACHINES INSTEAD OF HOW TO RUN THE MACHINES.

WARS GOT BIGGER AND BIGGER AND FINALLY KILLED EARTH. THAT'S WHAT THE SILENT RADIO MEANS. THAT'S WHAT WE RAN AWAY FROM.

YOU'RE YOUNG. I'LL TELL YOU THIS AGAIN EVERY DAY UNTIL IT SINKS IN.

NOW WE'RE ALONE. WE AND A HANDFUL OF OTHERS WHO'LL LAND IN A FEW DAYS. ENOUGH TO START OVER. ENOUGH TO TURN AWAY FROM ALL THAT BACK ON EARTH AND STRIKE OUT ON A NEW LINE--

151

A NOTE ABOUT THE AUTHOR

RAY BRADBURY IS A WRITER OF MYSTERIES, SCIENCE FICTION, HORROR, FANTASY, AND MAINSTREAM FICTION, AND IS WIDELY CONSIDERED ONE OF THE GREATEST AND MOST POPULAR AMERICAN WRITERS OF THE TWENTIETH CENTURY. HE HAS WRITTEN NOVELS, SHORT STORIES, PLAYS, POETRY, SCREENPLAYS, AND TELEPLAYS. MANY OF HIS WORKS HAVE BEEN ADAPTED FOR TELEVISION AND FILM.

HIS MOST POPULAR BOOKS ARE THE NOVELS *FAHRENHEIT 451* AND *SOMETHING WICKED THIS WAY COMES,* AND THE STORY COLLECTION *THE MARTIAN CHRONICLES.* SINCE HIS WORK WAS FIRST PUBLISHED IN THE 1940s, BRADBURY HAS RECEIVED MANY AWARDS. AMONG THESE ARE A SPECIAL CITATION FROM THE PULITZER PRIZE BOARD IN 2007 FOR HIS "DISTINGUISHED, PROLIFIC, AND DEEPLY INFLUENTIAL CAREER AS AN UNMATCHED AUTHOR OF SCIENCE FICTION AND FANTASY." HE HAS ALSO RECEIVED THE NATIONAL MEDAL OF ARTS, A WORLD FANTASY AWARD, THE SCIENCE FICTION AND FANTASY WRITERS OF AMERICA GRAND MASTER AWARD, AND AN EMMY AWARD, AMONG OTHERS.

MORE INFORMATION ABOUT THE AUTHOR, HIS CAREER, AND HIS CURRENT PROJECTS CAN BE FOUND AT WWW.RAYBRADBURY.COM.

A NOTE ABOUT THE ARTIST

DENNIS CALERO ATTENDED THE NEW WORLD SCHOOL OF THE ARTS IN MIAMI, THEN STUDIED ARCHITECTURE AT THE PRATT INSTITUTE IN BROOKLYN, BEFORE SWITCHING TO ITS ILLUSTRATION PROGRAM AND STUDYING COMIC BOOK ILLUSTRATION AND CONTINUITY. ALONG WITH KRISTIN SORRA IN 1995, CALERO CREATED ATOMIC PAINTBRUSH TO PROVIDE COMPUTER COLORING FOR MARVEL AND DC COMICS, AND ACCLAIM ENTERTAINMENT. THIS CREATED AN OPPORTUNITY FOR COMMISSIONED POSTERS FOR MARVEL COMICS AND VARIOUS PROJECTS FOR AOL TIME WARNER AND SONY.

AFTER A NUMBER OF YEARS PAINTING BOOK COVERS, HE RETURNED TO COMICS ON MARVEL'S HARVEY AWARD-NOMINATED *X-FACTOR* (2006). HE ILLUSTRATED A RUN OF *LEGION OF SUPERHEROES* FOR DC COMICS, AND HIS GRAPHIC ADAPTATION OF *FRANKENSTEIN* FOR STONE ARCH BOOKS WAS A JUNIOR LIBRARY GUILD SELECTION. HE RETURNED TO MARVEL FOR THE ACCLAIMED X-MEN NOIR SERIES, DOING INTERIOR ART AND A WELL-RECEIVED SERIES OF COVERS.